Before the ABCs

Promoting School Readiness in Infants and Toddlers

by Rebecca Parlakian

ZERO TO THREE
Washington, D.C.

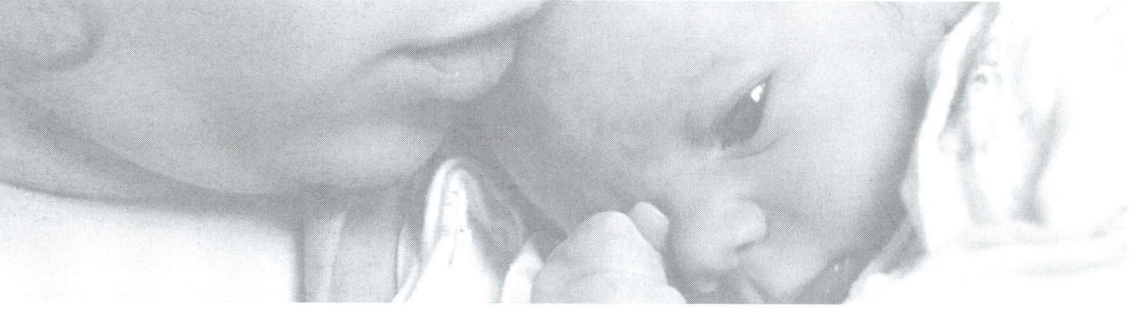

Acknowledgments

We gratefully acknowledge The David and Lucile Packard Foundation, whose leadership support has launched the Center for Program Excellence and its publications. We also extend our thanks to the W. Clement and Jessie V. Stone Foundation for generous support of the Center's work.

ZERO TO THREE Reviewers

Monimalika Day, Ph.D.
Linda Eggbeer, M.Ed.
Lynette Kimes, M.S.
Stefanie Powers, M.S.
Nancy L. Seibel, M.Ed., NCC

Expert Reviewers

Bruce Grellong, Ph.D., Institute for Infants, Children and Families of the Jewish Board of Family and Children's Services
Samuel Meisels, Ed.D., President, Erikson Institute
Marilyn M. Segal, Ph.D., Director of the Family Center at Nova University, Fort Lauderdale, FL

ZERO TO THREE

Suite 200
2000 M Street, NW
Washington, DC 20036-3307

http://www.zerotothree.org

Copyright © 2003 by ZERO TO THREE.
All rights reserved.

ISBN 0-943657-69-5

Cover photo: © Marilyn Nolt

Suggested citation:

Parlakian, R. (2003). *Before the ABCs: Promoting school readiness in infants and toddlers.* Washington, DC: ZERO TO THREE.

Additional copies of this monograph are available from ZERO TO THREE.
Call 800-899-4301 or visit our Web site at http://www.zerotothree.org

> We all have the duty to call attention to the science and seriousness of early childhood cognitive development—because the [years] between birth and age five are the foundation upon which successful lives are built.
>
> *—Laura Bush, White House Summit on Early Childhood Cognitive Development, July 26, 2001 (in Early Childhood-Head Start Task Force, 2002, p. iii)*

Introduction

Most parents of 5-year-olds, as they watch chubby hands clutching brand-new backpacks, think of starting school as their children's first step into the world of education and learning. These kindergartners, though, have already experienced a period of amazing growth and change during their first 5 years of life. Their relationships and experiences during this time have offered them important opportunities not just for learning, but for learning how to learn. These are the lessons that will help—or hinder—their ability to approach school with hope and optimism.

Increasingly, the goal of ensuring that all children are "ready for school" has become a national priority. As a result, programs that support children's school readiness are becoming more and more important to funders, policymakers, and parents alike. Preparing children for school requires two equally important sets of skills: the social-emotional skills necessary to communicate, cooperate, and cope with challenges and the cognitive skills that provide children with specific subject-based knowledge (e.g., letters and numbers).

Cognitive development—which includes the development of literacy and numeracy skills—is a crucial part of preparing children for school. But organized instruction is not necessary for infants and toddlers. In truth, the everyday activities and experiences of young children provide ample opportunity for infusing learning into play. Cognitive development is the natural product of warm and loving families, experienced and well-trained caregivers, and enriching environments.

This publication, designed for infant/family program leaders, examines the important role that both cognitive and social-emotional skills play in ensuring that children are ready for

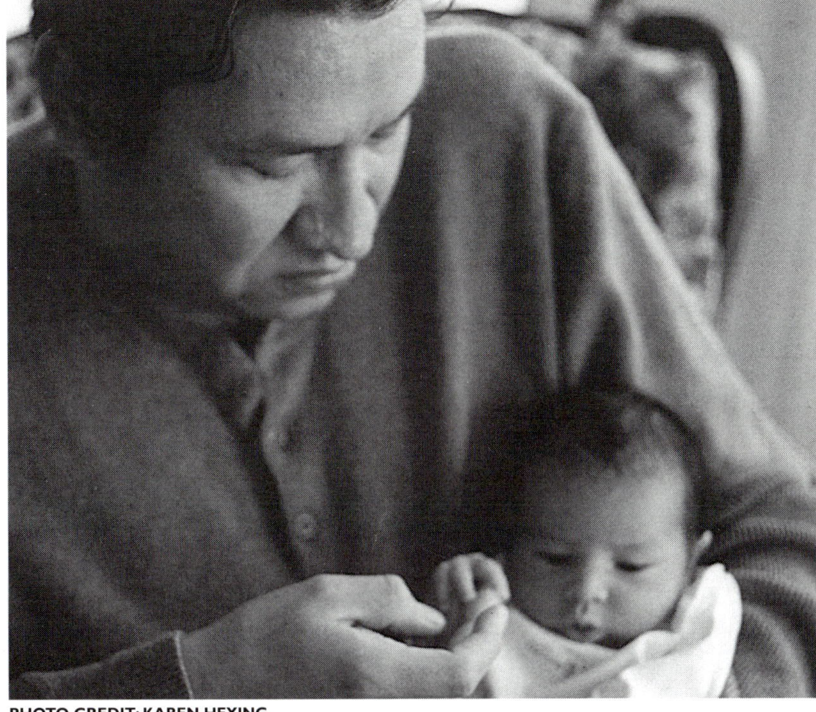

PHOTO CREDIT: KAREN HEYING

school. By exploring what school readiness means in the context of work with very young children, program leaders can better understand how they can support the lifetime learning of infants and toddlers in their communities. The material is divided into the following sections.

- **What Is School Readiness for Infants and Toddlers?** defines the concepts of school readiness and social-emotional development, and explains how they are linked.
- **How Very Young Children Learn** discusses how infants and toddlers construct knowledge in the context of relationships and through everyday routines and experiences.
- **Early Literacy Skills in Infants and Toddlers** outlines the process by which children develop pre-reading and language skills.
- **Early Numeracy Skills in Infants and Toddlers** presents some ways in which to help children develop foundational mathematics skills.
- **Social-Emotional Skills Make the Difference in School Readiness** highlights the crucial role that social-emotional skills play in school readiness, successful adjustment to school, and school success.
- **How Does Culture Affect Development?** explores the influence culture has on very

young children's development as well as on relationships between staff members and families.

- **Critical Connections: Linking Relationships and School Readiness** examines how relationships at all levels of the program (with supervisors, staff, and families) affect children's readiness to learn.

What Is School Readiness for Infants and Toddlers?

> [It is] in the first weeks and months of life ... that children first try to understand and master their environment, and find those efforts encouraged—or not; first attempt to concentrate and find it possible—or not; first conclude the world is orderly and predictable—or not; first learn that others are basically supportive and caring—or not. It is in those years that the foundations for later learning are laid down. Or are not. (*Heart Start*, 1992, p. 4)

School readiness and school success are more than the result of acquiring a set of facts and skills. To be ready for school—and to succeed once there—requires a "secret ingredient": social-emotional skills. Development in the social-emotional domain refers to children's growing ability to experience, regulate, and express emotions; form close and secure interpersonal relationships; explore the environment; and learn—all in the context of family, community, and cultural expectations (ZERO TO THREE Infant Mental Health Task Force, 2001). These skills and abilities allow children to resolve conflict, persist when faced with challenges, cope with frustration, build friendships, and manage their emotions in appropriate ways. Because children's cognitive and social-emotional skills develop in concert, promoting school readiness means supporting learning in both these areas.

Babies are born ready to learn. Adults encourage this capacity by providing very young children with the experiences and nurturing relationships they need. This ensures that they will develop the skills that are related to their later success in school and in life.

Seven Critical Social-Emotional Skills to Support School Readiness

In 1992, ZERO TO THREE identified the seven most critical social-emotional competencies for school-ready children. These characteristics (listed below) equip young children with knowledge more fundamental than numbers or letters; they provide very young children with the knowledge of "how to learn" (*Heart Start*, 1992).

1. **Confidence** is a sense of control and mastery of one's body, behavior, and world. Children feel likely to succeed at their undertakings and expect adults to be helpful.

   Brianna (14 months old) has begun taking her first unsteady steps. Her mother is encouraging her efforts: "Go on, sweetie! You can do it!" Brianna takes a few more steps; her bright smile showing how proud she is of this accomplishment. "Wow, Brianna, you're walking! That's great," says her mom, giving her a big hug and kiss.

2. **Curiosity** is the sense that finding out about things is positive and leads to pleasure.

   Curtis' home visitor brought a new pop-up book with her today. Curtis (9 months old) is fascinated by it, opening and closing the pages and laughing at the brightly colored pop-ups. All during the visit, he shows a strong preference for this book among the many available in his home visitor's bag. She sits by while he and his mother cuddle and read it together, lingering over his favorite pictures and laughing at the funny pop-ups.

3. **Intentionality** is the desire and ability to have an impact, and the determination to act on that desire with persistence; an internal drive or emotion is expressed outwardly through an action or communication. This skill is related to feeling competent and effective. For children with special needs, the outward expression of intentionality may vary from what is expected of typically developing children.

   Eleni (4 months old) couldn't quite roll over yet. But she tried and tried and tried. She rolled onto her side, she reached out with her arms and tried to get the momentum to flop over onto her tummy. Her parents encouraged her, giving her lots of room to play and explore and telling her with words and

touch that she was doing well. At 5 months, she rolled over and, beaming with pride, rolled over again and again.

4. **Self-control** is the ability to modulate and control one's own actions in age-appropriate ways; a sense of inner control.

   Alex (2 years old) was angry—the building blocks area was full! He banged his truck on the floor again and again. When his caregiver came to see what was wrong, Alex pointed to the children building towers and, as his eyes filled with tears, said, "Blocks!" His caregiver scooped him up in a hug and agreed, "Sometimes it's frustrating when we can't play with our favorite toy right away. But look, nobody is playing with the bristle blocks right now—let's build with those!" Alex took a deep breath and smiled. That sounded good.

5. **Relatedness** is the ability to engage with others based on the sense of understanding and being understood by others.

   Marissa (3 years old) saw the new girl at child care start to cry when her mommy dropped her off. Marissa thought for a minute and then patted the newcomer's back. "Why you sad?" she said.

6. **Capacity to communicate** is the desire and ability to exchange ideas, feelings, and concepts with others—verbally or otherwise. This skill is related to feeling trust in others and pleasure in engaging with others, including adults.

   "Hi, Davis! Hi there!" said his occupational therapist, Janeen. "Aiiii! Aiiii!" said Davis (6 months old), waving his arms. "Your whole body is saying hello, isn't it? How was your weekend? I missed you, little guy." Davis babbled happily in response, turning his body so he could look in Janeen's eyes and moving his arms and legs. "Davis, I love hearing your voice," says Janeen, "How about you tell me more while we play?"

7. **Cooperativeness** is the ability to balance one's own needs with those of others in a group activity.

   It was Circle Time. Colleen (16 months old) was playing with the xylophone. She didn't want to go to the circle yet. Her teacher, though, continued signaling to the children that it was time to transition by calling out "Circle Time, Circle Time" and ringing a bell. Colleen banged the xylophone a few more times, then put it on the shelf. She made her way over to the circle and sat down where she always did, on the pink square.

Think for a moment about specific ways your program helps babies and toddlers to develop these competencies—either through activities or ways of being with the children. Jot them down here.

How Our Program Helps Very Young Children Become Ready for School

Confidence:

Curiosity:

Intentionality:

Self-control:

Relatedness:

Capacity to communicate:

Cooperativeness:

Social-emotional skills influence how children understand the world, how they construct their perception of self, and whether they come to know relationships as satisfactory and fulfilling. How children approach new people, places, and challenges is, in large part, defined by their social-emotional competence. These skills pave the way for school success.

Other Ways to Think About School Readiness

The term *school readiness* is commonly used to describe the constellation of academic skills (i.e., specific subject-based knowledge, like letters and numbers) and other abilities that children ideally possess when they enter school. These domains typically include those listed below (National Education Goals Panel, 1997?; "School Readiness," 2000).

- **Approaches to learning:** inclination to use skills and knowledge; capacities such as enthusiasm, curiosity, and persistence; temperament and cultural values
- **Language development and communication:** verbal language and literacy skills
- **Cognition and general knowledge:** typically understood academic skills, such as the knowledge of shapes and spatial relations, number concepts, the assignment of particular letters to sounds
- **Physical well-being and motor development:** health status, growth, abilities and disabilities, gross and fine motor skills

Although the topic is beyond the scope of this publication, *school readiness* also implies an important reciprocity: children must be ready for school, and schools must be ready for young children. To fulfill their role, teachers must possess several skills (Ahearn, Nalley, & Marsh, 2000):

- knowledge of the growth and development of typically and atypically developing children;
- knowledge of children's strengths, interests, and needs (and the ability to individualize their approach based on that knowledge);
- knowledge of the social and cultural contexts in which children and their families live; and
- the ability to translate developmental knowledge into practice.

To promote young children's academic success, schools must be prepared to meet the needs of individual children, ideally allowing children to work at their own pace on learning experiences that are active and hands-on, initiated by children, and supported by teachers (National Association for the Education of Young Children, 1995).

How Very Young Children Learn

Jessica's father lowered her into a tub filled with warm water. Jessica (9 months old) immediately reached for the bright orange starfish toy floating in the tub and started chewing on it. As her dad lathered up a washcloth, he started to sing their special bath song. "Head and shoulders, knees and toes," he sang, reaching to tickle her toes with the washcloth. Jessica giggled and kicked her feet. Her dad continued, "Eyes and ears and mouth and nose. . . ." He kissed the tip of her nose. Jessica laughed and cooed and kicked some more.

In infants and toddlers, all domains of development are interrelated. Each is a thread in the same cloth; pull one, and the others follow. In the vignette above, Jessica shows signs of her social and emotional development in the way that she has fun with her father and trusts him to keep her safe in the tub. Her communication skills are evident in the way that she "tells" her dad that she likes the song by kicking, cooing, and laughing. She is developing gross (large-muscle) and fine (small-muscle) motor skills when she kicks the water or picks up the slippery starfish and puts it in her mouth. Her intellectual abilities grow when she sees the cause and effect of kicking her legs and feeling the water splash; when she hears that songs have a logical, regular rhythm; and when she "feels" (through tickles and kisses) that words like "nose" and "toes" represent parts of her body.

Learning for infants and toddlers happens in the context of relationships. Jessica's father lets her know how much he enjoys spending time with her by singing and talking to her. By doing this, he supports her social and emotional development. When he responds to her efforts to communicate, he tells Jessica that she is worth listening to and has important things to say. By using their "special song" each time he gives her a bath, he helps Jessica understand the world is a logical, dependable, ordered place. Through her father's words and actions—in the context of their relationship—Jessica comes to know that she is a good person, fun to be with, and an effective communicator. This knowledge makes her feel loved and secure and will help her

develop other positive relationships as she grows.

Learning in very young children takes place through play, the active exploration of their environment, and most importantly, through interactions with the significant adults in their lives. Infants and toddlers learn best when they feel competent and the people around them reinforce their worth. They learn best when the learning is fun, when it happens during the normal course of the day, and when it emerges from the world around them. And very young children learn best when they are able to follow their interests—that is, when play is directed not by adults but by the children. Research shows that rather than needing to be pushed to learn, children enter the world ready to learn as part of their "genetic equipment"; they are driven to learn to walk, talk, explore the world through their senses, love, and be loved (B. Bowman, 2001).

Starting with Strengths: Supporting the Development of Very Young Children

Children enter infant/family programs at different levels of social-emotional, cognitive, and physical development. Over the first 3 years, these skills develop at different rates in different children—one child may have a large vocabulary but lagging motor skills, and another might be quick and coordinated in physical games but have difficulty making friends. As staff and parents think about children's strengths and challenges, they should be encouraged to identify competency in terms of these interconnected domains of development.

Read the vignettes below. Identify some of the children's strengths and challenges. How can their strengths be used to support development in the areas they find more challenging?

Katelynn (3 years old) is a chatterbox with a large vocabulary. She is very creative and loves symbolic play, especially dress-up. She always chooses the queen's crown. In fact, the need to always be the "queen" is pretty typical of her. Despite her engaging, witty personality, Katelynn is rather bossy and has difficulty entering play with other children. She tends to tell everyone what to do, resulting in the group dispersing—only to reconvene in another play area without her. How could you support Katelynn's creativity while helping her to learn more cooperative play and social skills?

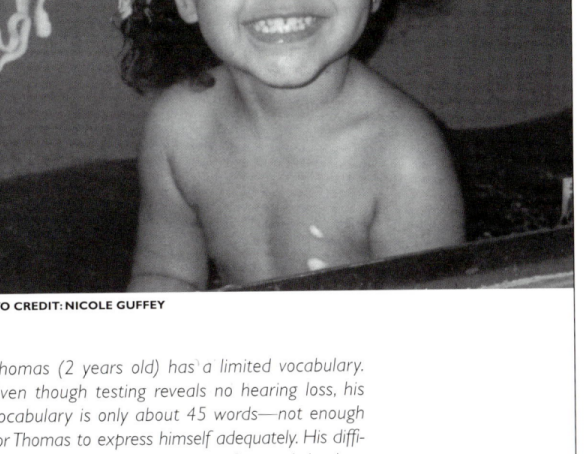

PHOTO CREDIT: NICOLE GUFFEY

Thomas (2 years old) has a limited vocabulary. Even though testing reveals no hearing loss, his vocabulary is only about 45 words—not enough for Thomas to express himself adequately. His difficulty with verbal communication frequently leads to feelings of frustration, which he tends to express physically through biting. In an effort to make himself understood, Thomas has been quick to imitate gestures and movements and has developed his own gestures to request food and indicate other wants. Thomas is a charmer, with a good sense of humor. Knowing his strengths, how could you assist his language development?

Janni (7 months old) was referred into her county's early intervention home visiting program as a result of delays reported by her foster mother. Janni's home visitor notes that her motor skills are slightly delayed; for example, she doesn't yet roll over. What causes her home visitor more concern is that Janni doesn't seem to have the desire to roll over—she doesn't show an interest in making an impact on the world around her. She is a sweet, cooperative baby with an easygoing, flexible temperament.

What more would you want to find out about Janni to better understand her strengths and challenges? What could you suggest to help encourage Janni's desire to roll over as well as develop the strength and coordination to do so?

Think of a child you (or one of your staff) work with. Jot down the child's strengths and any areas that might be challenging for him or her. What are some creative ways you can use this child's strengths to address the challenges you've listed? How can you encourage further development of those strengths ?

Why Not Flash Cards?

> You can't make children ready for 3rd grade by treating 2- and 3-year-olds like 3rd graders. (Lally, 2001)

It is possible to introduce cognitive skills such as literacy and numeracy during the infant and toddler years (see pages X–X). Rote learning, flash cards, and one-size-fits-all approaches, however, are developmentally inappropriate for very young children. The risk of early instruction is that drill and practice may actually reduce children's natural curiosity and enthusiasm for the learning process and so undermine their interest in learning. Toddlers who feel pushed to read, for example, may become frustrated and fearful, and begin to associate those negative feelings with books. Although introducing emergent literacy and numeracy skills is important, these abilities are unlikely to flourish in very young children when presented out of context as isolated skills (National Association for the Education of Young Children, 1995). Rather, infants and toddlers learn best when the adults in their lives introduce opportunities for exploration and creative play into their everyday routines and interactions.

> "Infants and toddlers learn best when they feel competent and the people around them reinforce their worth."

Early Literacy Skills in Infants and Toddlers

Parents and others (e.g., funders and policymakers) commonly view school readiness and early literacy as one and the same. However, early literacy is only one part of what makes children school-ready. Early (or emergent) literacy is what children know about reading and writing before they can actually read and write. It encompasses all the experiences—good and bad—that children have had with books, language, and print from birth onward. Because these experiences unfold in the context of relationships, they are linked to and dependent on social-emotional development.

Early literacy evolves from several behaviors and skills developed during the first 3 years of life. Understanding these "prerequisites" help direct service professionals better understand the various milestones that children pass along the path to literacy. The four early literacy behaviors for infants and toddlers follow (Shickedanz, 1999).

1. **Book handling behaviors:** physical manipulation or handling of books, such as page turning and chewing
2. **Looking and recognizing:** paying attention to and interacting with pictures in books (e.g., gazing at pictures or laughing at a favorite picture); recognition of and a beginning understanding of pictures in books (e.g., pointing to pictures of familiar objects)
3. **Picture and story comprehension:** understanding pictures and events in a book (e.g., imitating an action seen in a picture or talking about the events in a story)
4. **Story-reading behaviors:** verbally interacting with books and demonstrating an increased understanding of print in books, such as babbling in imitation of reading or running fingers along printed words

Language development provides the foundation for the development of literacy skills. Speaking, reading aloud, and singing all stimulate children's understanding and use of language. In addition, it is by listening to others

and speaking to themselves that children develop phonological awareness, that is, recognizing and understanding important attributes of spoken language (e.g., that *bag, ball,* and *bug* all start with "b"). Research has shown that phonological awareness and phonemic awareness (understanding that spoken words are made up of separate sounds) predict how quickly children learn to read (Armbruster, Lehr, & Osborn, 2002, p. 8). Most importantly, however, expressive language (spoken speech) helps children to communicate—to make a request, protest or complain, greet or take leave of someone, respond to a comment, ask a question, solve a problem, and share their feelings and ideas (Weitzman & Greenberg, 2002, p. 34–35). Being able to communicate—and being understood by those around them—is a powerful achievement for very young children.

Language development occurs gradually during the first 3 years of life and, indeed, throughout childhood. The table **Seven Stages of Communication and Language Development** describes the development of expressive language skills from birth to age 3.

The skills of speaking, reading, and writing are reciprocal and interactive, each supporting the others' development. For example, toddlers engaged in symbolic play (when they pretend that one object represents another, like using a block as a car) are poised to understand that letters can represent sounds and vice versa. Babbling, talking, looking, and listening prepares babies and toddlers to want to—and be able to—later learn to recognize letters, read, and write.

These capacities unfold in the context of relationships. Supportive, nurturing relationships provide children with a safe place within which to explore. Often this exploration is embedded in play. Consider Allie's and Carmen's experiences below. Which child is likely to have better feelings about books?

Allie's caregiver handed her a chunky board book. Allie (9 months old) immediately started chewing on the pages, then began to open and close the book repetitively. She stopped for a moment to look at a page with an interesting picture of a dinosaur before beginning to bang the book on the floor, all the while joyfully saying, "Bu bu bu!" Her caregiver sat next to her, rubbed her back every so often, helped her hold the book open to the page she wanted to look at, and responded to her babbles by saying, "It's a good book, isn't it?"

PHOTO CREDIT: REBECCA PARLAKIAN

Carmen (2 years old) and his caregiver are sitting near the center's bookshelf. His caregiver picks one of his favorites to read before naptime. Carmen, meanwhile, is stacking chunky board books to make a tower. "Nope, no more playing. Come on, let's read," she says. Carmen, though, is less interested in hearing the story than in playing with the book itself. He keeps grabbing for it, trying to hold the book. His caregiver gently pushes his hands away. Carmen then starts to squirm, reaching again for the book. "Mine!" he says. "Me read!" He grabs the book and starts to quickly turn the pages. "No, no," says his caregiver, annoyed. "Be gentle with the book! Don't grab at the pages. Here, give it back to me." She takes the book and puts it away. Maybe a lullaby will work better, she thinks.

These vignettes emphasize the importance of the caregivers' ability to recognize and support early literacy behaviors in very young children. Although both caregivers wanted to encourage

Seven Stages of Communication and Language Development (Weitzman & Greenberg, 2002, pp. 37–57)

Stage	Age	Communication skills
1	0–3 months	• Produce reflexive responses (e.g., crying, fussing, looking, smiling) to physical needs • Perform actions without a goal in mind (because they don't yet know that their behavior can affect others and make them behave in certain ways); however, caregivers respond as if babies *have* communicated intentionally: "Oh, you're hungry!"
2	3–8 months	• Show interest in others and want their attention, but don't yet communicate intentionally (still don't realize that they can send a message to make something happen) • Use facial expressions (e.g., smiling back at a smiling face) • Babble and make other vocalizations • Reach for, move toward, or look at objects or people of interest • Understand nonverbal cues such as gestures and intonation
3	8–13 months	• Communicate intentionally and become very sociable • Use conventional gestures (e.g., pointing, nodding) to communicate • Use sounds as if they were words (e.g., "Guh!" for "Look!") and imitate adult sounds • Begin question-asking through use of rising intonation • May start to use a few simple words
4	12–18 months	• "Crack" the language code: use a small number (10–50) of single words, usually for familiar people and objects • Use simplified versions of adult words (e.g., "baba" for bottle) • Persevere if not understood initially by repeating the message or finding another way to express their need or want
5	18–24 months	• Use two-word sentences • Increase vocabulary (to about 200 words) • Use negatives ("No," "Not") • Ask questions • Begin to take part in "real" (but brief) conversations • Understand simple directions and can answer simple questions
6	24–36 months	• Use three- to five-word sentences • Increase sentence length • Improve speech by becoming more grammatically correct—using prepositions, pronouns, verbs, plurals, etc. • Begin to ask, "Why?" • Tell stories • Participate more fully in conversations; understand two-step directions • Understand that a pause in conversation is a signal to respond

Note. Adapted from "Learning Language and Loving It" (pp. 37–57), by E. Weitzman and J. Greenberg, 2002, Toronto, Ontario, Canada: Hanen Centre. Copyright 2002 by the Hanen Centre. Adapted with the permission of the Hanen Centre.

an interest in reading, their words, feelings, and actions sent important—but very different—messages about books to the children in their care. Through interactions with adults, children can be encouraged or discouraged to seek out new learning experiences. Infants and toddlers may play with books and other literacy materials in ways that may not reflect adults' ideas of how they "should" be used. Regardless, children should be encouraged to explore literacy materials freely, in ways that are interesting to them. In this way, the 6-month-old mouthing a book leads to a 1-year-old stacking the books like blocks, to a 2-year-old who requests the same story over and over, to a 3-year-old who acts out the plot. By using all domains of development and all their senses, children develop the foundational skills necessary for a love of reading and a love of learning.

Early Numeracy Skills in Infants and Toddlers

Although definitions of *numeracy* vary, it is typically understood to mean "the ability to use appropriate mathematical knowledge, ... skills, ... and experience whenever they are needed in everyday life" (Perry, 2000). Research on early numeracy is rare compared with the extensive work done in the field of early literacy. Why is that? Several possibilities exist. First, from the Piagetian perspective, children's quantitative abilities before age 6 or 7 are believed to be "rudimentary and therefore of little interest" (D. C. Geary, 1994, p. 4, in Lefevre, 2000). (Jean Piaget is a noted cognitive-development theorist.) There also exists a "widespread belief that mathematical literacy is not as important as verbal or written literacy" (Diezmann & Yelland, 2000, p. 47). Although this area of children's cognitive development is less well understood than early literacy, early numeracy experiences (e.g., counting, sorting, recognizing shapes) are ubiquitous in early childhood, and the ability to use and understand numeracy concepts is necessary even for very young children.

Early mathematical concepts and skills—those which the 1st-grade mathematics curriculum builds upon—include (B. T. Bowman, Donovan, & Burns, 2001)

- recognition of size, shape, and patterns;
- ability to count verbally (first forward, then backward);
- recognition of numerals;
- ability to identify more and less of a quantity; and
- mastery of one-to-one correspondence (i.e., matching sets, or knowing which group has four and which has five).

Many children enter kindergarten already possessing some or all of these foundational math skills. According to a study by the National Center for Education Statistics, 94% of first-time-to-school kindergartners were able to read numerals, recognize shapes, and count to 10 (B.

Promoting Early Literacy in Your Program

This activity can be used in any infant/family setting, in home-based or center-based work. Spread a selection of books on the floor in front of a small group of children (or even one child). (Note: Sturdy board books or soft padded books are best). Observe how the children interact with the books. (Are they flipping them back and forth, stacking them like blocks, or pretending that they are sandwiches at a restaurant?) First, simply observe the children. Then, after you understand where the play is going, get involved—participating in, narrating, or otherwise adding to the children's play. For example, copy the children's actions, or describe their play with language: "Flip-flop! Open, shut, open, shut!"

Later, discuss the following questions:

- In what ways did the children play with the books?
- How did the children react to this play? What did they say? What did they do?
- What were their expressions? Did they enjoy it? How could you tell?
- Did any of their ways of using the books surprise you? Why?
- How did you feel about the children playing with books this way? Why do you think you felt that way?
- After the play ended, did the children return to the books later in the day? How did they play with them?
- Did the children show more, less, or the same amount of interest in seeking out books after this activity? Try repeating this activity several times a week, and continue to monitor the children's interest level in books.

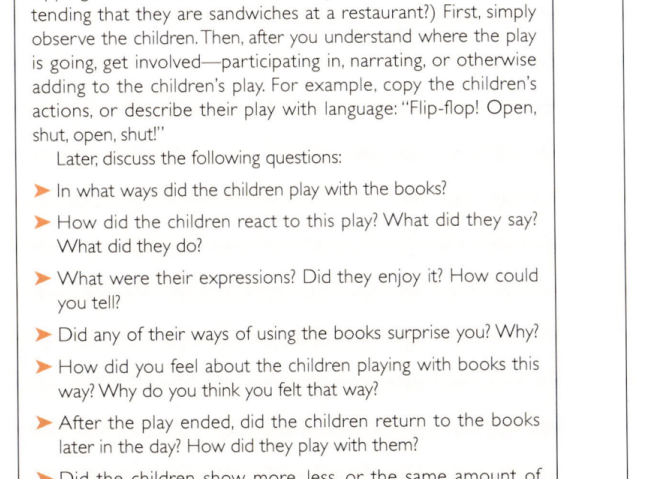

T. Bowman et al., 2001). True mathematical literacy, however, goes beyond content knowledge (such as being able to count or understand the difference between a triangle and square) to include conceptual knowledge. *Conceptual knowledge* refers to one's ability to extend and apply math skills to solve a problem. The four concepts explained below are the key components of mathematical literacy, and as with reading and language, there are ample opportunities to introduce these ideas during the first 3 years (Diezmann & Yelland 2000, pp. 49–52).

> "Important numerical concepts can be learned through everyday experiences."

- **Representation:** finding ways to express mathematical concepts with words, diagrams, pictures, symbols, and manipulative objects (like blocks)

  Casey (2 years old) was helping his mother get ready for lunch. His mother said: "Here's one napkin for Mommy, one for you, and one for your sister. One, two, three—3 napkins!"

- **Performing mathematical manipulations:** using the appropriate calculations and procedures, and using information given to answer the question posed

  Yvette (3 years old) and Sharlotte (30 months old) were standing in the center's outside play area and crying. When their caregiver, Julia, came over to see why, Yvette explained: "No trikes!" Julia watched several children zooming around on tricycles. "Hmmmm, we need more trikes, you're right. How many more?" Yvette shouted, "One for me and one for Sharlie!" Julia said, "That's right. We need two trikes for you and Sharlie. Let's see if anyone is done riding them yet."

- **Reasoning:** assessing a problem using facts, properties, and relationships to make and test conjectures, develop logical arguments, and identify a useful answer

  Carl (9 months old) looked at the toy his early interventionist brought that day. It was a plastic drum with three holes in the top. The holes were in the shape of a triangle, a circle, and a square. Carl looked at the blocks surrounding him. They, too, were different shapes. Carl picked up a triangular block. He put it in his mouth, then banged it on the floor. He touched the edges with his fingers. Then he tried to stuff it in each of the holes of the new toy. Surprise! It fell inside the triangle hole! Carl reached for another block, a circular one this time ....

- **Problem solving:** thinking through an issue; using prior knowledge and skills to reach and validate a solution (and realizing more than one solution may exist); posing one's own problems

  Jennie (18 months old) was given a bag of crackers. "Give everybody one," said her caregiver, Teri. Jennie gave each child at the table a cracker. But there was one left over. "What should we do with the extra cracker?" asked Teri. Jennie stopped and thought. Then she popped the cracker in her mouth!

In all of these examples, numeracy, language, and social skills come together. Children's ability to communicate effectively and express their ideas is integral to success with a given mathematical problem, whether it comes up in play (e.g., only five children may be in the blocks area at once) or in a more structured setting. Even seemingly nonmath activities like storytelling build numeracy skill by helping children develop sequencing skills that will later prove important to understanding mathematical concepts. And early numeracy experiences, though important in and of themselves, also provide ample opportunities to develop and extend children's vocabulary and literacy skills.

Very young children's social environments include exposure to counting systems ("Let's count the steps while we walk upstairs") as well as the principles of one-to-one correspondence ("Are there enough cookies for each child?") Most children develop an innate understanding of addition and subtraction through everyday interactions (Thomas has two shovels; Joseph wants one; after sharing, Thomas sees that he has one left) (B. T. Bowman et al., 2001). Important numerical concepts can be learned through

everyday experiences, such as matching (when choosing socks to wear) and counting (when counting out apples at the grocery store). Family members and other adults support children's number learning and emergent literacy skills through songs like "One, Two, Buckle My Shoe" and stories like *The Three Bears*. This informal foundation in mathematics, forged during very young children's prior-to-school years, provides a rudimentary conceptual framework from which formal instruction can begin.

How are early literacy and early numeracy skills different? Once children are able to "decode" letters, sounds, and grammatical rules, literacy acquisition is a matter of more of the same—expanding and extending vocabulary, grammatical knowledge, and reading comprehension (Lefevre, 2000). The various domains of mathematics skill, though based on the same basic knowledge, splinter off into distinctive disciplines with "many separate avenues and specific competencies"; in other words, geometry is very different from statistics, which is different from trigonometry (Lefevre, 2000). Numeracy, in its many incarnations, provides children with a lifetime of opportunities to find mathematical areas that they enjoy and in which they excel.

Social-Emotional Skills Make the Difference in School Readiness

> Current policies regarding education and job training are based on fundamental misconceptions about the way socially useful skills embodied in persons are produced. By focusing on cognitive skills as measured by achievement or IQ tests, they exclude the critical importance of social skills, self-discipline and a variety of non-cognitive skills that are known to determine success in life.
>
> —James J. Heckman, Ph.D., Nobel Laureate in Economic Sciences (Heckman 2000)

Research suggests that social-emotional skills are critical to ensuring a smooth transition to kindergarten (Peth-Pierce, 2000). When children arrive at kindergarten on their first day, teachers usually have some basic expectations for their classes: that children can listen and follow directions, are interested in toys and tasks, and are able to start and finish small projects. It is children's social-emotional literacy that gives them the skills they need to meet these expectations. A positive adjustment to kindergarten is an important achievement; children who are not successful in the early years of school often fall behind from the start (Peth-Pierce, 2000).

Children's social-emotional skills—and the impact that difficulties in this domain have on learning—are not an issue for future debate but a real day-to-day challenge for today's teachers. Recently surveyed kindergarten instructors note that *half their class or more* enters school exhibiting the following characteristics that make their transition to school challenging (M.J. Cox, S. E. Rimm-Kaufman, & R. C. Pianta, 2000, in Peth-Pierce, 2000, p. 2):

- difficulty following directions (46% of respondents),
- difficulty with individual work (35% of respondents),

- difficulty with group work (30% of respondents),
- problems with social skills (20% of respondents), and
- immaturity (20% of respondents).

Each of these items is connected to the development of children's social-emotional skills in the years preceding school. And the influence of these skills doesn't stop after kindergarten. Over the long term, difficulty with social-emotional skills puts children at risk for early school failure, poor academic outcomes later in school, and difficulties in the workplace as adults (Peth-Pierce, 2000).

What Attributes Make Children Socially and Emotionally Ready for School?

Well-developed social-emotional skills ease the adjustment to kindergarten. Listed below are some of the attributes that support children's school readiness (Peth-Pierce, 2000, p. vii).

- Confident
- Friendly
- Develops relationships with peers and teachers
- Communicates well with teachers and peers
- Concentrates on tasks
- Persists at challenging tasks
- Effectively communicates emotions
- Listens to and responds to instructions
- Pays attention

Another research study on school readiness surveyed parents and teachers on the "early warning signs" of preschool difficulty. Neither group mentioned the lack of traditional pre-academic skills (e.g., knowledge of letters, numbers, and colors) as a "red flag" for preschool success. Rather, they all cited the development of more basic skills—self-control, respect for others, a sense of confidence and competence—as integral to a successful school transition and agreed that basic skills created a potential stumbling block (Center on Families, Communities, Schools and Children's Learning, 1994). In this way, social-emotional skills consistently serve as an important predictor of children's ability to participate positively in their education, whether in preschool or kindergarten.

Kindergarten is a crucial year in children's development, as they experience the transition to an educational environment. Social-emotional skills play an important part in paving the way for a successful first year of school. Research has shown that the quality of children's relationships with their kindergarten teachers predicts how well those children adapt and learn, that year and the next (B. Bowman, 2001). In addition, at the end of the kindergarten year, the children who were considered to have made a positive adjustment to school also had the most friends, were able to maintain these friendships over time, and established new friendships across that first year (G. W. Ladd, 1990, cited in National Education Goals Panel, n.d.). Thus, early skills in relating well to others—evidenced in the ability to form meaningful connections to both peers and teachers—are critical prerequisites for school readiness and successful adjustment to school.

Children who lack crucial social-emotional skills struggle to transition successfully during the kindergarten year. Because they have limited skills in this area, these children often engage in fewer positive social interactions and receive less support from peers in kindergarten and experience a greater incidence of problems with later behavioral, academic, and social-emotional development (Peth-Pierce, 2000). "Emotional disturbance," the fourth-most-common diagnosis among 6- to 11-year-old children receiving special education services (6% of students this age), may well result from inadequate early development of social-emotional skills (Ounce of Prevention Fund). Over the long term, early academic difficulty is a risk factor for delinquent and antisocial behavior, and grade retention is a predictor for dropping out of school and adolescent pregnancy (Peth-Pierce, 2000).

Social-emotional skills are an integral part of school readiness because they give very young children the skills they need to communicate, cooperate, and cope in new environments. They help children to adapt and be resilient, to resolve conflict, to make sense of their feelings, and to establish a network of supportive, satisfying relationships to depend on and grow within. Social-emotional skills allow children to concentrate on learning.

Supporting School Readiness: What Role Does Adults' Self-Awareness Play?

Identifying our own beliefs about literacy and school readiness helps us to understand why parents, supervisors, or colleagues might feel strongly about particular educational goals, approaches, or activities. To explore your own beliefs about school readiness, take a few moments to complete the sentences below. You might want to discuss your reactions with your supervisor or co-workers, perhaps in a staff meeting or training session.

- The best way to help a baby learn to talk is …
- With regard to academic skills, parents should …
- Parents want to help their children …
- Before they start kindergarten, all children should know how to …
- Educational toys are …
- The role of play is …
- Children should know how to read by age …
- When children are having trouble acquiring a new skill, parents should …

Gather in a small group with colleagues to discuss your responses. As you listen, think about some more questions:

- What life experiences, beliefs, or assumptions might underlie your responses to these questions?
- How does your field or academic background influence how you view school readiness issues?
- What role might your family, cultural, or ethnic background play in your beliefs about preparing children for school?

How Does Culture Affect Development?

The word *culture* conjures up many meanings. We use it to refer to the shared implicit and explicit rules and traditions (expressed through the beliefs, values, and goals) of a group of people (Kalyanpur and Harry, 1999). Culture is a fundamental part of children's developing identity. It provides the context within which all learning takes place, during their first 3 years and throughout their lives.

Cultural identity is shaped by a family's national or ethnic background and includes much more, as well. Culturally based values, assumptions, and beliefs are formed through the experiences people have with school, community, professional, and social groups. Socioeconomic class also contributes to one's cultural identity. Each family has its own culture that reflects its shared history, experiences, and beliefs. For this reason, beliefs about discipline, the value of school, and appropriate behavior, for example, may vary dramatically even within families from the same ethnic, national, or racial backgrounds. A supportive, nurturing family relationship system that permits individuals to develop to their fullest potential is the most important protective factor for the healthy development of very young children. These familial relationships, which exist within the context of a community and societal culture, provide children with the solid social-emotional grounding they need to approach school with confidence, optimism, and enthusiasm for learning.

Professional discipline is another cultural lens; it influences how staff members and leaders understand a family's particular situation. For example, an occupational therapist might be most concerned with the fact that a very young boy can't sit up on his

Thoughts on Early Intervention Services

An important lesson to draw from the entire literature on successful early interventions is that it is the social skills and motivation of the child that are more easily altered—not IQ. These social and emotional skills affect performance in school and the workplace. We too often have a bias toward believing that only cognitive skills are of fundamental importance in life.

—*James J. Heckman, Nobel Laureate in Economic Sciences 2000 (Heckman 2000)*

own, but his mental health therapist may be most concerned that the same child bites when he's frustrated.

It is worthwhile to examine how one's own culture, professional discipline, and education have influenced beliefs about children's development and readiness for school. Although more research needs to be conducted to examine how children from different cultures develop socially and emotionally, it is possible—even likely—that direct service professionals may have expectations of "normal" or "developmentally appropriate" behavior different from those of the families they serve. It is always crucial for staff members to gather information about children and their families from various sources over a period of time, and to seek out additional information about the family's culturally based norms and perceptions. This knowledge helps professionals take into account the diversity within and among families of varied cultural backgrounds. Most importantly, assessors must understand what they themselves bring to the process. How does their culture—professional, personal, racial, and ethnic—affect what they see and hear?

Culture in Practice: Responding to Challenging Behaviors

Reports of problem behaviors in kindergarten vary by race and ethnicity, and the pattern of these differences depends on who rates the children's behavior. Teachers typically report more African American than White and Asian children as exhibiting problem behavior in their classrooms. However, parents rating their own children's behavior tend not to report misbehavior along racial or ethnic lines (West, Denton, & Germino-Hausken, 2000).

Ask staff to reflect on challenging children in the program. Is their behavior the result of

- difficulty the children are experiencing, or difficulty in the children's lives?
- the children's temperaments, or mismatches between the children's and the professionals' temperaments?
- the professionals' cultural beliefs or past experiences?
- a combination of these issues, or another variable?

These are tough questions. It may be helpful to seek outside support and assistance in exploring issues of this nature. Some approaches include

- asking colleagues to observe interactions with the children and then offer feedback;
- videotaping (with parents' permission) interactions with the children and then discussing the tape with staff;
- talking with parents, and soliciting their thoughts and ideas;
- consulting with a child development expert or mental health professional; or
- observing the children and keeping records of the their behavior over several days to determine whether issues occur at a particular time (e.g., after lunch or before naptime) or in response to some other variable.

For program leaders and their staff, working with diverse families and colleagues to promote young children's school readiness raises challenges. Staff members may discover culturally based differences among themselves related to issues of school readiness. These differences can enrich the program's services if they are recognized, negotiated, and addressed. No one person can expect to know all about every culture's values, beliefs, and assumptions about child rearing and school readiness for young children. However, all staff members can learn to recognize and share their own culturally based beliefs and attitudes, to listen carefully to others, and to work together to negotiate differences when necessary. Young children and their families—as well as leaders and staff—benefit when their cultures are honored, respected, and included in the program's delivery of services.

Resolving Cultural Dilemmas

The following three vignettes explore various issues related to culture and infant/family work. Use the reflective questions that follow the vignettes in group discussions, training sessions, or one-on-one meetings with staff members.

Vignette 1: Aziz

Aziz (18 months old) just started child care. His caregiver, Carla, was shocked when his mother explained that taking daily walks was too much for a toddler. She asked Carla to carry Aziz or put him in the stroller. In his family's culture, one important way that parents nurture their children is by holding them and keeping them close, even into the toddler years. Carla felt both irritated ("Doesn't this mom know that I care for three other kids? You put one in the stroller and everyone else wants a ride!") as well as perplexed ("Isn't it true that being able to walk for short distances helps children develop motor skills and a sense of independence and self-esteem?").

Questions to think about:

- If you were Carla, what would you do or say to better understand this situation?
- Based on this brief vignette, what are the differences in cultural values between Carla and Aziz's mother?
- Think of a time when a difference in cultural beliefs created a dilemma for you on the job. How did you respond? Would you respond the same way, if you had the chance to do things over? If not, why not?

Vignette 2: Madison

The early intervention team for Madison, a 3-year-old with a moderate hearing loss, was meeting to discuss her goals for the coming year. Each professional spoke briefly about Madison's accomplishments to date, her strengths, and the areas that require continued attention. Madison's speech therapist was excited. "I have to admit I was really reluctant at first to meet with Madison at her child care center. I thought it would be too distracting, but it's really working out well." Madison's father was thrilled. "So you're helping her to talk to the other kids?" The speech therapist looked confused for a moment. "Well, in the long run. But for our weekly sessions, I've arranged to meet in a room down the hall." Madison's father rolled his eyes. "That's not the point of having you come to the center. We want her to be able to talk to the other kids, to make friends. You're not helping her do that when you take her out of the room!" Madison's mother spoke up as well. "We don't care if she sounds perfect. All that matters is that she's able to play with other kids, that they understand her. What are you going to do about that?"

Questions to think about:

- If you were Madison's parents, how would you feel during the discussion above?
- How can occupation or field act as a cultural "lens" through which one perceives what children and families might need? What beliefs about child rearing have you developed through your work?
- If you were a member of Madison's early intervention team, how would you respond to her mother's question?

Vignette 3: Ariel

Each time Jim, a home visitor, went to the Hawkins' apartment to work with Ariel (11 months old), he experienced a dilemma. There were some things about the house that he thought were not in Ariel's best interest. For example, the window shades were always pulled, making the apartment very dark, and Ariel was routinely placed in a bouncy seat in front of the television. Jim's initial impulse was to make recommendations for changes, but he first wanted to learn more about why Kendall (Ariel's mother) kept the room that way. He started the conversation with a simple observation. "I notice that when I come here you always have the shades down." Kendall nodded, "That's because we live on the first floor. To feel safe in this neighborhood, I keep the shades down so nobody can look in. And the TV's on so anyone who walks through the alley knows there's someone home." Jim then addressed Ariel's need for movement and an opportunity to actively explore her surroundings. He suggested that, rather than sitting in her bouncy seat, during their next visit, Ariel play on the floor. Kendall looked concerned. "I know that's important and everything, but I can't put her on the floor because of the roaches" (adapted from Zeitlin & Williamson, 1994)

Questions to think about:

- If you were Jim, how would you respond to Kendall's comments?
- What assumptions did Jim have about good environments for children when he started this conversation with Kendall?
- Do you think this vignette describes a dilemma due to cultural differences? Why or why not?

Critical Connections: Linking Relationships and School Readiness

The Role of Parent–Child Relationships

Parents are the most important people in children's lives. They serve as role models in the acquisition of social-emotional skills. Research shows that parents' beliefs about the appropriate ways to express emotion, resolve conflict, persuade, and cooperate with others have a profound influence on toddlers' abilities to get along with peers, follow rules, and cooperate with adults—and ultimately, to be ready for school and become active, caring citizens (Center on Families, Communities, Schools and Children's Learning, 1994). What children experience early and regularly with the adults who care for them forms their understanding of themselves and the world. For example, children who experience loving interactions, safely explore, and depend on stable routines learn important lessons: that they are lovable and important and that the world is a good place. A child's view of herself—whether smart and capable or stupid and inept—becomes the lens through which she sees and understands all new social interactions.

> "The parent–child relationship also helps set the tone for children's relationships with teachers."

Study after study in the field of attachment confirms the great importance of supportive, nurturing relationships during the first 3 years of life. Research results reveal that children who had received less sensitive care as babies and toddlers (Hawley, 1998)

- were at significantly higher risk for poor developmental outcomes,
- experienced difficulty in forming relationships with peers in preschools and early adolescence,
- showed decreased levels of school achievement,
- were more likely to require special education services,
- exhibited more behavior problems, and
- were more likely to use drugs and alcohol in adolescence.

Additional research indicates that children who were maltreated during the first few years of life tend to be more anxious, inattentive, and apathetic than other children and aggressive and withdrawn in social settings. The most neglected children demonstrate the most severe difficulty in school and the poorest performance. In total, 65% of the sample were either retained or referred for special education services by the end of their first year of school (*Heart Start*, 1992).

The parent–child relationship also helps set the tone for children's relationships with teachers. For example, children's experiences in positive, satisfying relationships with parents help them establish positive, secure relationships with preschool teachers (DeMulder, Denham, Schmidt, & Mitchell, 2000). This crucial achievement is an important predictor for a successful transition to early education environments (B. T. Bowman et al., 2001).

When infants and very young children receive what they need from their parents, they learn to believe that the world is a good place; that it is safe to explore; and that loving adults will provide comfort, affection, and security. Children who don't receive this loving care spend a great deal of energy trying to ensure that these needs are fulfilled by someone, sometime. How much energy do these children have left for learning, exploration, and for the new concepts and challenges that are a part of going to school?

The Role of Staff–Child Relationships

One of the most important accomplishments of a child's first year is establishing a close, nurturing bond with a parent or other primary caregiver. Children also develop meaningful relationships with other adults in their lives, like a

child care or mental health professional, occupational therapist, or home visitor. Although the parental relationship is always primary, children's attachments with other adults can strengthen the parent–child bond as well as offer the more opportunities for children to experience supportive, nurturing relationships. Such relationships with parents and others have been associated with greater self-confidence and self-motivated learning during the toddler years (Center on Families, Communities, Schools and Children's Learning, 1994). As in parental relationships, when these interactions are supportive, responsive, and nurturing, children begin to develop trust, empathy, compassion, generosity, and a conscience. Research shows that healthy adult–child relationships provide a context for supporting children's growing sense of self-direction, curiosity, persistence, cooperation, caring, and conflict resolution (Greenough et al., 2001). These social-emotional skills help children first to approach school with confidence and optimism, then to successfully adjust to the academic environment.

The adults that populate the lives of very young children—family members and the professionals who support them—make important contributions to children's school readiness. For infants and toddlers, care and education are not separate activities. They occur together, one leading to the other, one supporting the other. According to one study on school readiness,

> If there is a single critical component to quality, it rests in the relationship between the child and the teacher/caregiver, and in the ability of the adult to be responsive to the child. But responsiveness extends in many directions: to the child's social, emotional and physical characteristics and development. (B. T. Bowman et al., 2000, p. 16)

Children start kindergarten with 5 years of accumulated life experiences. Because each set of experiences is unique, children have different perspectives on education, different approaches to relationships with adults and peers, and different levels of competency with social-emotional and academic skills. The ability of direct service professionals to individualize their approach to specific children and families is crucial to ensuring that services are meaningful and effective.

PHOTO CREDIT: NANCY GUADAGNO

The Role of Program Leaders

Imagine every child's ideal: All of the adults in his life support him, help him, love him, and keep him safe. When these people are working together—sharing information, listening to and supporting one another, and learning from one another—the baby flourishes. Now imagine the opposite. Without supportive, responsive relationships among parents and professionals (and between professional colleagues), less energy and attention is available for the baby.

Relationships between supervisors and staff members are influenced by the relationships that staff have with children and families. The effect of this *parallel process* extends throughout the program and the families served. Supportive, respectful staff–supervisor relationships help staff members establish effective partnerships with parents. In turn, parents learn to relate to

Partnering With Parents: It's All About the Relationship

Think of a parent who has approached you with a concern about his or her child, the program, or its services. Ask a colleague to role-play this interaction with you. Don't feel bound to the response you offered originally. If you'd like to respond differently, go ahead. Ask yourself the following questions:

- What issue did the parent raise?
- Do you think that that issue is the "real" issue? If not, why?
- What is your relationship with this parent?
- How did this interaction make you feel when it happened?
- How did those feelings influence your response?

When you have finished the exercise, discuss with your partner

- how the role play felt,
- what you learned from re-visiting this interaction,
- how you modified your response (if you did), and
- why you modified your response (if you did).

their children in supportive, respectful ways. (Note: A negative influence also can propagate throughout the system.)

Effective leaders ensure that staff members are not left alone to respond to the challenging situations and emotions that arise in their work with families. Rather, leaders provide staff a safe place to explore their questions, feelings, beliefs, and ideas. By using the "Look, Listen, Learn" model (below), leaders can help staff members develop greater self-awareness and an increased capacity for identifying the unique needs of a particular family.

- **Look:** Observe the staff member. What do you know about this individual's background, experience, and temperament? What unspoken messages are being sent—is she maintaining eye contact or using closed body language?
- **Listen:** Listen as the staff member describes an experience with a family. What is her perspective? How does she sound—excited, frustrated, resigned? Is her voice trembling, or softer or louder than usual?
- **Learn:** Learn from what you've seen and heard. Make a "best guess" as to what might be going on. Wonder about your staff member's needs and feelings. Identify goals for this interaction and decide what response from you would best support those goals—making a suggestion, observing something about the family that might have been missed, asking a question? As you receive more information, modify your best guess and your response.

The parallel process is a crucial, though often invisible, component in all staff–supervisor interactions. How leaders treat their team strongly influences how staff members treat families and children. When staff members feel supported in their work, with the safety to learn and grow, they are better able to approach families in the same way.

Supporting School Readiness: Recommendations for Staff Members

Staff members, in their daily interactions with children, play a crucial role in school readiness efforts. Normal routines, interactions, and activities between children and the important adults in their lives can be both the source and the genesis of innumerable learning opportunities. The following recommendations highlight specific ways that direct service professionals can support the development of very young children's school readiness skills.

✔ **Respond to children's individual needs and temperaments.** To provide responsive services, staff members must be able to adapt their approaches to meet different children's needs. To do this, staff must be excellent observers of children and search for the meaning behind infants' and toddlers' gestures, gurgles, cries, and glances. Responsive staff members wonder why particular behaviors occur, come up with educated guesses to explain why, and interact with children to determine whether their guesses are correct. (Is a crying baby tired? hungry? wet? lonely? frustrated?)

Staff in all infant/family fields can respond to children as individuals, build on their strengths, and support their development. Some examples of responsive care follow.

- A *home visitor* brings a book about dinosaurs and several dinosaur figurines because in a previous visit, Allan (3 years old) expressed great interest in dinosaurs.
- An *early interventionist* rearranges plans with Carl (18 months old), who isn't interested in grabbing and manipulating the bouncy balls that she brought that day but loves reaching for the bubbles his mother is blowing.
- A *child care teacher* helps the very shy Isabella (2 years old) to enter play with other children by suggesting she draw with the sidewalk chalk outside. A budding artist, Isabella is comfortable and confident when she is drawing and soon attracts a group of fellow creative spirits.
- An *infant mental health specialist* helps the parents of Tobias (6 weeks old) to understand their pediatrician's diagnosis of colic and see that his inconsolable crying in the evening is not a sign that he is unhappy (a concern of theirs). She then checks to see what their doctor suggested and asks if there are any follow-up appointments or referrals to a pediatric gastroenterology specialist. Learning of none, she discusses a few different ideas they may try to ease the baby's discomfort.

When staff members are responsive, they support children's social-emotional development and promote school readiness. Concrete ways to do this include

- building on children's interests by adapting the environment or activity;
- showing respect for children and allowing them to practice new skills;
- observing and documenting the development of children;
- fostering children's self-confidence and sense of self-efficacy through words and actions;
- modeling problem-solving strategies;
- helping children communicate their needs;
- encouraging children's natural curiosity and enthusiasm for learning;
- letting children know that adults are supportive, loving, and helpful; and
- assisting parents in responding flexibly to their children's needs.

✔ **Encourage children's curiosity and exploration.** If caregivers select all the "lessons" that are to be learned or provide an environment that is not stimulating, children will push to do what they are most interested in or to create their own stimulation. Often children are told "No," "Stop," or "Bad"—not because they are not learning, but because they are following their own learning agenda or searching for experiences that interest them. Although setting some limits is important and helps keep children safe, it is equally important to allow children to engage in self-directed learning, that is, to follow their interests and become immersed in new ideas. This approach supports their development of persistence, motivation, critical thinking, and logical thinking skills.

✔ **Introduce early literacy and numeracy concepts in developmentally appropriate ways.** A program that serves infants and toddlers can introduce literacy and numeracy concepts. Staff members can use these concepts in many ways that are fun, meaningful, and developmentally appropriate for very young children:

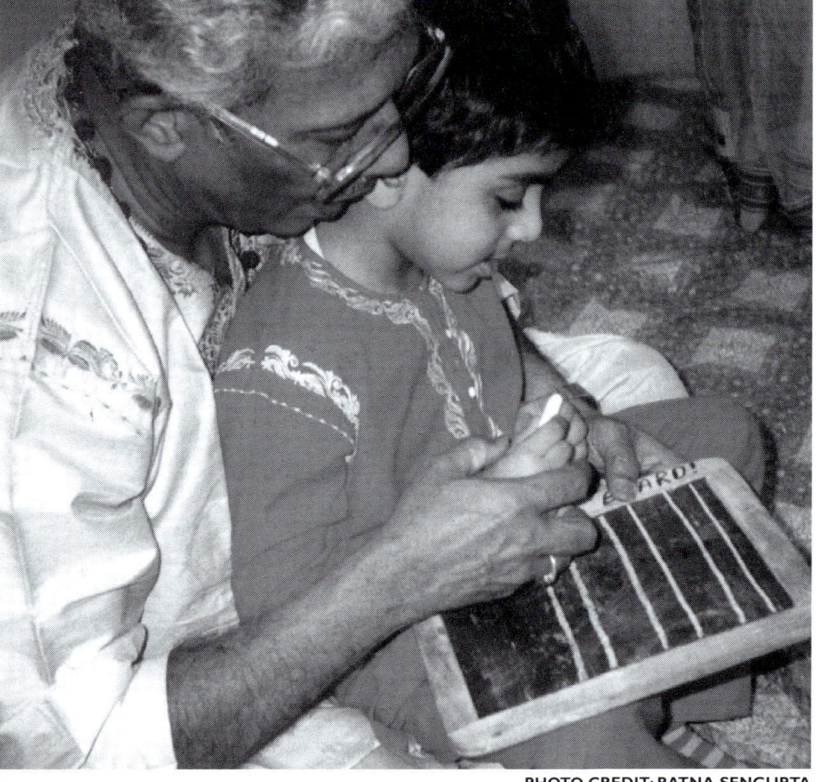

PHOTO CREDIT: RATNA SENGUPTA

- Help older toddlers count the number of blocks in the pile or the number of books on the shelf.
- Label items in the room in all of the languages used by the children.
- Teach concepts like "more" and "less" by pointing out things children see in the world around them ("That tree has more leaves than the one next to it").
- Help parents make books for their children using pictures from magazines or catalogs. (Note: This activity can be used with parents with all levels of reading ability because the book can be words and pictures, or just pictures.)
- Make magazines and newspapers available for parents to promote family literacy.

✔ **Appreciate the "magic of everyday moments."*** Children often develop social-emotional skills not in specially planned lessons but in the context of their daily interactions and experiences—napping, eating, playing, and diapering. When staff members use these everyday moments to support and expand children's current repertoire of social-emotional skills, they help prepare young ones to enter the larger world with all of its demands.

To help parents do the same, staff members should emphasize the important learning that takes place in everyday interactions (e.g., the give-and-take of parents imitating their babies' babbling teaches children about turn-taking and communication and, from a social-emotional perspective, that they are important, loved, and listened to). These observations also encourage parents' pride in and enjoyment of their children.

✔ **Establish strong working relationships with families.** Staff members can support children's school readiness through the relationships they establish with parents. When these interactions are open and collaborative, parents receive the support they need to learn and grow in their new roles as mothers and fathers. By extension, parents are better able to support their children's development with affection, responsiveness, and sensitivity. Staff members can look for opportunities to provide parents with an outlet to explore the questions and challenges associated with child rearing; wonder about their children's behavior, needs, and motivations; and brainstorm about how best to respond.

✔ **Recognize and respect family culture.** By entering a dialogue with parents about how they want their children raised and what family or cultural practices they value, staff let families know that they are respected partners in the program. When it is difficult to incorporate families' wishes into program practices, a solid foundation of respect and openness helps make negotiating these differences easier and more helpful for everyone.

✔ **Reduce parents' anxiety about school success.** A newborn does not need expensive "developmental" toys or flash cards to become intellectually curious and academically successful. Staff members can help parents understand

*The Magic of Everyday Moments™ booklets, a joint effort of ZERO TO THREE and the Johnson & Johnson Pediatric Institute, are available free of charge. Call 877-565-5465 or visit the ZERO TO THREE website (http://www.zerotothree.org/magic/).

that the foundation of school readiness is in supportive, nurturing relationships that provide children with a safe "home base" from which they can explore, learn, and grow. This close parent–child bond also helps children to develop the key social and emotional competencies that are necessary for a successful transition to school.

✔ **Provide anticipatory guidance.** When staff members help parents anticipate their children's developmental changes, parents are better prepared to support their children's learning. Armed with accurate information, parents can respond to their children's changing developmental needs in appropriate ways. Their ability to meet their children's needs contributes to a greater sense of competency and confidence, which in turn strengthens the family as a whole.

✔ **Support inclusive environments.** Very young children with special needs may have unique challenges in achieving the skills necessary to enter school—social-emotional or otherwise. Inclusion is an important intervention because it draws children with disabilities into the mainstream, where ongoing interactions with typically developing children may help support their development. Inclusion is also important for children whose development is more typical, because diversity helps them to broaden their experiences and learning and to develop empathy. By learning about children's strengths, challenges, and goals, staff members can play an important role in supporting their ongoing development during the first 3 years of life. Collegial, supportive, and respectful relationships among parents and all of the professionals involved in providing services to children with special needs are especially crucial.

Supporting School Readiness: Recommendations for Program Leaders

What role do leaders take in encouraging the development of children's social-emotional skills and getting them "ready for school"? Program leaders can enhance systemic support for children's school readiness by focusing on the four pillars of early learning: children, parents, teachers, and policymakers.

✔ **Promote children's development.** First and foremost, create an environment in which children and families feel accepted and understood. Programs can accomplish this goal by

- training staff members to provide responsive care that takes into account children's individual needs and temperaments;
- ensuring that services are provided within the context of families' home cultures;
- welcoming the opportunity to include children of all ability levels in program services;

> "School readiness goals must be appropriate to typical infant and toddler development."

- supporting staff members as they try to understand children's behavior;
- providing children with the opportunity to have a wide range of cognitive, motor, social, and sensory experiences; and
- encouraging staff efforts to create an emotionally supportive environment in families' homes by helping parents feel supported in their role, responding to parents' needs as individuals and as parents, and encouraging parents' own learning and development.

✔ **Involve parents.** Parent perspectives add a crucial ingredient to any discussion of program operations, services, and structure. To involve parents in meaningful and lasting ways, leaders might

- establish position(s) for a parent or parents on the board of directors;
- involve parents in the program's advisory committee;
- invite parents to participate in interviews of new staff members (including senior-level positions);

- encourage parents to contribute to staff and management performance reviews;
- solicit feedback from parents on the program's services through surveys or other means (e.g., one-on-one interviews);
- confer with parents about their children's individual interests, strengths, and needs; and
- request parental input in identifying appropriate activities, field trips, and ways to celebrate in your program.

✔ **Stay focused on what children and families need.** Program leaders remain constantly alert to new funding opportunities, and it can be tempting to make program changes based on available funding. Indeed, it is part of a program leader's job to ensure the financial solvency of the organization. At the same time, it is equally important to carefully consider how new funding opportunities relate to the program's expertise, mission, philosophy, and beliefs. It is also

Talking with Funders and Policymakers: Developing School Readiness Skills in Infants and Toddlers

✔ **Parents are central to children's development during the first 3 years of life.** Even the very best infant/family program cannot work alone. In addition to nurturing, stimulating early education environments, children need homes in which they are well-nourished, safe, and loved by family members. For this reason, it is crucial that infant/family programs support parents' efforts to meet their children's needs in the social-emotional, health, and cognitive domains. When parents feel supported and have access to the resources they need, they are better able to support their children's growth and development.

✔ **Close, nurturing bonds between children and their primary caregivers, established during the first year of life, are crucial to later social-emotional gains.** These gains include the development of trust, empathy, compassion, generosity, and conscience. Furthermore, such relationships provide a context for supporting the development of children's curiosity, self-direction, persistence, cooperation, caring, and conflict-resolution skills. In short, loving, caring interactions—with parents other adults—give children a strong emotional foundation from which they can approach learning with hope and optimism.

✔ **Social-emotional development during the infant and toddler years forms the foundation that allows traditional school skills—literacy and numeracy—to develop.** Without the ability to concentrate, persist with difficult tasks, communicate effectively, and establish relationships with others, children are at a serious disadvantage in the classroom.

✔ **School readiness goals must be appropriate to typical infant and toddler development.** Rote learning, flash cards, and one-size-fits-all approaches are developmentally inappropriate for very young children. For infants and toddlers, learning takes place through play and active exploration of their environment. Program leaders and staff members must reexamine the concepts of "learning" and "skill development" to ensure that their expectations are age appropriate for infants and toddlers. For example, in this age group, playing dress-up helps to build symbolic thinking and communication skills, and cause-and-effect toys (e.g., jack-in-the-box) help develop logical thinking.

✔ **In addition to promoting social-emotional development, programs can expose children to the traditional school readiness skills of literacy and numeracy.** Although these experiences are often disguised as play, they form the basis for how children perceive their own ability to learn and master new tasks. For example, supporting the development of early literacy skills in a 6-month-old may mean encouraging her to explore a chunky board book with her eyes, hands, and mouth. Even though she may end up chewing it, she is learning that books offer her a positive, rewarding experience.

wise to review the current research to ensure that there is a sound basis for the proposed changes and confirm that they are appropriate for very young children and their families.

✔ **Support staff members' development.** Some specific approaches include providing access to

- regular supervision designed to support staff in their efforts to relate effectively to parents and children;
- peer support and mentoring opportunities;
- the resources necessary to support school readiness goals, including curricula, toys, and resource and referral information for parents; and
- training on the development of very young children.

The power of well-trained staff members cannot be emphasized enough. Research shows that the professional development of teachers predicts the developmental outcomes for children, and the educational level of the caregiving adults remains a strong predictor of children's achievement (B. Bowman, 2001). In short, when parents, teachers, and caregivers are well-informed, children are likely to receive the cognitive and emotional support and the motivation they need for school success.

✔ **Develop self-awareness in staff members.** Using individual or group discussions, leaders can help staff members understand what they bring to the work. Like the families they serve, direct service professionals perceive the world in the context of their own beliefs, expectations, and assumptions. How do staff members' cultural, familial, and community experiences influence their interactions with children and parents?

✔ **Educate funders and policymakers on the needs of very young children.** In an era of tight budgets and limited funding, it is more important than ever to clearly articulate the link between social-emotional skills and school readiness to funders and policymakers. The box **Talking with Funders and Policymakers** (page 22) summarizes the relationship between children's social-emotional competence and their successful transition to school.

Conclusion

School readiness means that children are ready to learn. They enter the classroom able to form relationships with teachers and peers, to listen and communicate, to cooperate with others and cope with challenges, to persist when faced with difficult tasks, and to believe in themselves. These skills reflect children's social-emotional development.

Research shows that the influence of children's social-emotional development extends far beyond childhood. Social-emotional skills lay the groundwork for improved academic outcomes, better odds of later school and vocational success, an easier time developing rela-

tionships with peers, less reliance on social services, and higher earnings (Peth-Pierce, 2000, p. 2). The important relationship between school readiness and social-emotional development can be summarized in five key points (adapted from B. T. Bowman et al., 2001).

- Responsive, supportive relationships with parents, caregivers, and other significant adults nurture children's desire to learn.
- Learning requires a solid foundation of social-emotional skills.
- The development of social-emotional skills depends on and is responsive to experience.
- Children acquire new experiences within the context of relationships with the significant adults in their lives; for this reason, the education and care of infants and toddlers are "two sides of the same coin."
- Social-emotional development and academic achievement are united priorities. They represent a developmental continuum—a gathering-up of all the skills, abilities, and attributes that are needed to succeed in school and throughout life.

The first 3 years of life are characterized by rapid and amazing development in infants and toddlers. From birth to age 3, children form their first attachments to others and, through these interactions, learn to trust, communicate, and receive support and comfort. Leaders and direct service staff in infant/family programs can make a profound impact on children's social-emotional development (and, by extension, on the school readiness of those children) when they offer infants, toddlers, and their families the "Three R's": *responsive* services, *relationships* that are collaborative and nurturing, and *respect* for children's individual differences. Only then can infant/family programs truly reject the notion of children as passive participants in school readiness efforts and instead follow in the wake of a "curious, motivated, social child who is dying to learn" (Lally, 2001).

References

Ahearn, C., Nalley, D., & Marsh, C. (2000). *School readiness in North Carolina.* Greensboro, NC: SERVE.

Armbruster, B.B., Lehr, F., & Osborn, J. (2002, September). *A child becomes a reader* [Booklet]. Jessup, MD: National Institute for Literacy. Available from 800-228-8813.

Bowman, B. *Eager to learn.* (2001, December). Plenary presentation at the 16th Annual National Training Institute of ZERO TO THREE, San Diego, CA.

Bowman, B., Donovan, M.S., & Burns, M.S. (Eds.). (2000). *Eager to learn: Educating our preschoolers* [Executive summary]. Washington, DC: National Academy Press.

Bowman, B.T., Donovan, M.S., & Burns, M.S. (Eds.). (2001). *Eager to learn: Educating our preschoolers.* Washington, DC: National Academy Press.

DeMulder, E.K., Denham, S., Schmidt, M., & Mitchell, J. (2000). Q-Sort assessment of attachment security during the preschool years: Links from home to school. *Developmental Psychology, 36*(2), 274–282.

Diezmann, C., & Yelland, N.J. (2000). Developing mathematical literacy in the early childhood years. In N.J. Yelland (Ed.), *Promoting meaningful learning: Innovations in educating early childhood professionals* (pp. 47–58). Washington, DC: National Association for the Education of Young Children.

Early Childhood-Head Start Task Force. (2002, April). *Teaching our youngest: A guide for preschool teachers and child care and family providers* [Booklet]. Jessup, MD: U.S. Department of Education. Available from 877-433-7827. Retrieved March 13, 2003, from http://www.ed.gov/offices/OESE/teachingouryoungest/

Greenough, W., Emde, R.N., Gunnar, M., Massinga, R., & Shonkoff, J.P. (2001). The impact of the caregiving environment on young children's development: Different ways of knowing. *Zero to Three, 21*(5), 16–23.

Hawley, T. (1998). *Ready to succeed: The lasting effects of early relationships.* Washington, DC: Ounce of Prevention Fund and ZERO TO THREE.

Heart start: The emotional foundations of school readiness. (1992). Washington, DC: ZERO TO THREE.

Heckman, J. J. 2000. *Fostering human capital.* Chicago: Ounce of Prevention Fund and University of Chicago Harris School of Public Policy Studies.

Kalyanpur, M., and Harry, B. 1999. *Culture in special education: Building reciprocal family–professional relationships.* Baltimore: Paul H. Brookes.

Lally, R. *School readiness.* (2001, December). Plenary presentation at the 16th Annual National Training Institute of ZERO TO THREE, San Diego, CA.

Lefevre, J. (June, 2000). Research on the development of academic skills: Introduction to the special issue on early literacy and early numeracy. *Canadian Journal of Experimental Psychology/Revue canadienne de psychologie expérimentale, 54*(2). Retrieved October 17, 2002, from http://www.cpa.ca/cjep/edito_eng.html

Morisset, C.E. (1994, October). *School readiness: Parents and professionals speak on social and emotional needs of young children* (Report No. 26). Center on Fami-

lies, Communities, Schools and Children's Learning. Retrieved January 25, 2002, from http://readyweb.crc.uiuc.edu/library/1994/cfam-sr/cfam-sr.html

National Association for the Education of Young Children. (1995). *NAEYC position statement on school readiness.* Retrieved January 24, 2002, from http://www.naeyc.org/resources/position_statements/psredy98.htm

National Education Goals Panel. (n.d.). *Getting a good start in school.* Retrieved January 23, 2002, from http://www.negp.gov/Reports/good-sta.htm

National Education Goals Panel. (n.d.). *Reconsidering children's early development and learning: Toward common views and vocabulary.* Retrieved January 23, 2002, from http://www.negp.gov/Reports/child-ea.htm

Ounce of Prevention Fund. *Toward the ABCs: Building a healthy social and emotional foundation for learning and living.* Chicago: Ounce of Prevention.

Perry, B. (2000). *Early childhood numeracy.* Canberra, Australian Capital Territory: Commonwealth of Australia. Retrieved October 17, 2002, from http://www.aamt.edu.au/numeracy/perry.pdf

Peth-Pierce, R. (2000). *A good beginning: Sending America's children to school with the social and emotional competence they need to succeed* (The Child Mental Health Foundations and Agencies Network [FAN] Monograph). Bethesda, MD: The National Institute of Mental Health, Office of Communications and Public Liaison.

Schickedanz, J.A. (1999). *Much more than the ABCs.* Washington, DC: National Association for the Education of Young Children.

School readiness: Helping communities get children ready for school and schools ready for children. (2000, August). Washington, DC: Child Trends.

Weitzman, E., & Greenberg, J. (2002). *Learning language and loving it: A guide to promoting children's social, language, and literacy development.* Toronto, Ontario, Canada: The Hanen Centre.

West, J., Denton, K., & Germino-Hausken, E. (2000, February). *America's kindergartners: Findings from the Early Childhood Longitudinal Study, kindergarten class of 1998-99, fall 1998* (Publication No. 2000-070). Washington, DC: U.S. Department of Education, National Center for Education Statistics.

Zeitlin, S., & Williamson, G.G. (1994). *Coping in young children: Early intervention practices to enhance adaptive behavior and resilience.* Baltimore: Paul H. Brookes Publishing Co.

ZERO TO THREE Infant Mental Health Task Force. (2001, December). *What is infant mental health?* Washington, DC: ZERO TO THREE. Retrieved April 22, 2003, from http://www.zerotothree.org/imh/

Additional Resources

Barbarin, O.A. (2002). Culture and ethnicity in social-emotional and academic development. In *Set for success: Building a strong foundation for school readiness based on the social-emotional development of young children* (pp. 45–61). Kansas City, MO: The Ewing Marion Kauffman Foundation.

Copley, J.V. (2000). *The young child and mathematics.* Washington, DC: National Association for the Education of Young Children.

DeVries, R., & Kohlberg, L. (1987). *Constructivist early education: Overview and comparison with other programs.* Washington, DC: National Association for the Education of Young Children.

Espinosa, L.M. (2002). The connections between social-emotional development and early literacy. In *Set for success: Building a strong foundation for school readiness based on the social-emotional development of young children* (pp. 30–44). Kansas City, MO: The Ewing Marion Kauffman Foundation.

Fromboluti, C.S.,& Rinck, N. (1999). *Early childhood: Where learning begins—mathematics.* Washington, DC: U.S. Department of Education. Retrieved October 17, 2002, from http://www.ed.gov/pubs/EarlyMath/title.html

Greenspan, S.I. (with Lieff Benderly, B.). (1997). *The growth of the mind—and the endangered origins of intelligence.* Cambridge, MA: Perseus Books.

Jablon, J.R. (1992). Mathematics in early childhood. In A. Mitchell & J. David (Eds.), *Explorations with young children: A curriculum guide from The Bank Street College of Education* (pp. 177–188). Mt. Rainier, MD: Gryphon House.

Katz, L.G. (1987). *What should young children be learning?* Retrieved January 24, 2002, from http://readyweb.crc.uiuc.edu/library/pre1990/katz87.html

Katz, L.G. (1991). *Readiness: Children and schools* (Report No. EDO-PS-91-4). Retrieved January 24, 2002, from http://ericeece.org/pubs/digests/1991/katz91.html

Knitzer, J. (2001). *Building services and systems to support the healthy emotional development of young children: An action guide for policymakers.* New York: National Center for Children in Poverty.

National Center for Early Development and Learning. (1998, September). *Assessing readiness.* Retrieved January 24, 2002, from http://fpg.unc.edu/~ncedl/PAGES/spotlt3.htm

Nurss, J.R. (1987). *Readiness for kindergarten.* Retrieved January 24, 2002, from http://readyweb.crc.uiuc.edu/library/pre1990/nurss87.html

Raver, C. Cybele, & Knitzer, J. (2002). *Ready to enter: What research tells policymakers about strategies to promote social and emotional school readiness among three- and four-year old children.* New York: National Center for Children in Poverty.

Thompson, R.A. (2002). The roots of school readiness in social and emotional development. In *Set for success: Building a strong foundation for school readiness based on the social-emotional development of young children* (pp. 8–29). Kansas City, MO: The Ewing Marion Kauffman Foundation.

To order more copies of this publication or other ZERO TO THREE Infant Mental Health publications, please call us toll-free at 1-800-899-4301 or visit us online at http://www.zerotothree.org.

Center for Program Excellence

Funded by:
The David and Lucile Packard Foundation
W. Clement and Jessie V. Stone Foundation

ISBN 0-943657-69-5